What Does a
SUPREME
COURT JUSTICE Do?

David J. Jakubiak

PowerKiDS
press

New York

To Doug Brown, whose judgment I admire

Published in 2010 by The Rosen Publishing Group, Inc.
29 East 21st Street, New York, NY 10010

First Edition

Editor: Amelie von Zumbusch
Book Design: Julio Gil
Photo Researcher: Jessica Gerweck

Photo Credits: Cover Charles Ommanney/Getty Images; pp. 5, 21 Paul J. Richards/AFP/Getty Images; p. 6 Robyn Beck/AFP/Getty Images; p. 9 Joe Raedle/Getty Images; p. 10 Brendan Smialowski/Getty Images; p. 13 © AP Images; p. 14 Mark Wilson/Getty Images; p. 17 Shutterstock.com; p. 18 Ed Clark/Time Life Pictures/Getty Images.

Library of Congress Cataloging-in-Publication Data

Jakubiak, David J.
  What does a Supreme Court justice do? / David J. Jakubiak.
    p. cm. — (How our government works)
  Includes index.
  ISBN 978-1-4358-9361-0 (library binding) — ISBN 978-1-4358-9818-9 (pbk.) — ISBN 978-1-4358-9819-6 (6-pack)
  1. United States. Supreme Court—Officials and employees—Juvenile literature.
  2. Judges—United States—Juvenile literature. I. Title.
  KF8742.J35 2010
  347.73'26—dc22
                                        2009031547

Manufactured in the United States of America

CPSIA Compliance Information: Batch #WW10PK: For Further Information contact Rosen Publishing, New York, New York at 1-800-237-9932

CONTENTS

THE HIGHEST COURT

On May 26, 2009, President Barack Obama chose Sonia Sotomayor to fill an opening on the Supreme Court. The selection made history. Sotomayor was the first Latina picked for the highest court in the land.

The pick was closely watched because of the power of the Supreme Court. The Court can throw out or uphold laws. Everyone in the United States must follow the Court's rulings. Even the lives of children can be changed by the Supreme Court. Its rulings have changed where some children go to school. It has also changed what kids learn while they are there.

Sonia Sotomayor (left) was sworn in as a member of the Supreme Court on August 8, 2009. As all justices do, she promised to treat people equally.

John Roberts became the chief justice in 2005. On January 20, 2009, Roberts (right) swore Barack Obama (left) in as president.

THE JOB OF THE SUPREME COURT

In 1787, leaders from across the newly formed United States met to establish a government. They set up three branches so that power would be spread around. **Congress**, the legislative branch, makes laws. The executive branch carries out laws. The judicial branch rules on laws. The Supreme Court is at the top of the judicial branch.

Congress sets the number of justices. At first, there were six. Over time, the number changed several times. In 1869, Congress made the last change, settling on nine justices.

The Supreme Court is made up of nine judges, called justices. There are eight associate justices and one chief justice. The chief justice has special duties, such as giving the **oath** of office to the president.

BECOMING A JUSTICE

A Supreme Court justice is picked by the president and voted on by the **Senate**. The Senate holds meetings to learn about the person chosen for the Court. This person answers questions from senators about his or her beliefs. Once on the Supreme Court, justices keep their positions until they **retire** or die.

The people presidents pick do not always make it to the Supreme Court. In 2005, President George W. Bush picked Harriet Miers for the Court. Some senators argued she should not become a Supreme Court justice because she had never been a judge. A few weeks later, President Bush took her name out of consideration.

President George W. Bush picked Samuel Alito, seen here, for the Court. He was sworn in on January 31, 2006, after answering many questions from senators.

In 2006, lawyers for Massachusetts, seen here, brought a case to the Supreme Court. They wanted the U.S. government to do more to stop pollution.

A CASE FOR THE SUPREME COURT

In 1967, Mildred Jeter and Richard Loving asked the Supreme Court to make their marriage lawful. At the time, Virginia law said their marriage was not legal because Jeter was black and Loving was white. The Supreme Court threw out the Virginia law.

After reviewing a request to hear a case, the justices vote. If four of the nine justices agree to hear a case, it goes before the Court.

Every state has courts. There is also a national court system. Cases begin in lower courts and can be **appealed** to higher courts. The Supreme Court is the country's highest court. Its justices choose to hear only very important cases. These cases often deal with rights given by the U.S. **Constitution**.

ARGUING BEFORE THE COURT

When the Court takes a case, the parties in the case write arguments called **briefs**. If they think that the lower court made the right decision, their brief will say why. If they believe that the lower court was wrong, they will list the reasons that they think so.

After briefs are **filed**, each side comes before the nine justices to state their case. During these arguments, the justices can ask questions. Some Supreme Court justices, such as Antonin Scalia, are known for asking many hard questions. Others, such as Clarence Thomas, generally just listen to the arguments.

This drawing shows lawyer Walter Dellinger arguing a case for Washington, D.C., before the Supreme Court in 2008. The city wanted to ban certain guns.

In this picture from 2006, Justice Stephen Breyer (back left) and Justice Clarence Thomas (back right) talk. The Court's justices do not always agree.

HOW RULINGS ARE MADE

In the 1960s, teacher Susan Epperson took the state of Arkansas to court over its law against teaching **evolution**. The case ended up in the Supreme Court. In 1968, all nine justices ruled, or voted, in her favor.

The Court's ruling is offered in an opinion written by a justice who voted for the winning decision. Other justices can write opinions agreeing or disagreeing with the Court's ruling.

After they hear the arguments on both sides of a case, justices talk about the case. These **conversations** are private. Then, the justices rule on the case. They can agree with a lower court's decision, send a case back to a lower court, or change a decision. Rulings are read in court and sent out in writing.

A HOME FOR THE COURT

Today, visitors to Washington, D.C., can visit the Supreme Court building. However, the Court did not have its own home until 1935. Before that, the Court met in different parts of the Capitol.

The Supreme Court building is known for its huge **columns**. The columns are made out of a strong stone called marble. Cases are heard in the courtroom on the first floor. The first floor also has **chambers** for the justices. Some surprises can be found in other parts of the building. For example, there is a place to wash clothes in the basement. The fourth floor even has a basketball court!

The words "Equal Justice Under Law" are cut into the stone of the Supreme Court building. They remind people of the Court's important job.

In 1954, Thurgood Marshall (center) argued for the rights of African-American children. In 1965, he became the first African-American Supreme Court justice.

18

A LANDMARK DECISION

Supreme Court decisions have changed history. One such ruling came in the 1954 case *Brown v. Board of Education*. The case was brought by the parents of several African-American children. It was named after one of these children, an eight-year-old Kansas girl named Linda Brown. Brown was not allowed to go to a school near her house because she was African American.

In 1896, the Supreme Court had ruled that having separate services for black people did not deny anyone their rights. This time around, the justices disagreed. They ruled that having separate schools for African Americans was against the Constitution.

JUSTICES WHO CHANGED HISTORY

There have been many important Supreme Court cases. The Court's justices help shape our world. Justice Louis Brandeis served between 1916 and 1939. He believed strongly that people had a right to free speech and privacy. As chief justice from 1953 to 1969, Earl Warren's Court offered rulings that helped all people get equality under the law.

Justice Sandra Day O'Connor was picked by President Ronald Reagan in 1981. She was the first woman on the Court. Serving between 1981 and 2006, O'Connor was known as an independent justice. People were never sure how she would vote on a case.

Justice Sandra Day O'Connor has said that she tried to be "a fair judge and a hard worker." Today, she teaches kids about the importance of the judicial branch.

YOUR SUPREME COURT

In recent years, the Court has ruled on things like voting rights and how people running for government office can raise money. Many of these decisions have come down to close votes, separated by just one or two justices. Today, the Court is changing. In 2005, John Roberts became the youngest chief justice in over 200 years. Several new other justices have joined the Court since 2005, too. As older justices retire, more change will come. Each year brings several dozen new cases for the Court. You can use newspapers or the Internet to track new opinions and find out about the cases being considered.

GLOSSARY

appealed (uh-PEELD) Asked a judge in a higher court to take a second look at a legal decision.

briefs (BREEFS) Written arguments for cases that are presented in court.

chambers (CHAYM-burz) Offices.

columns (KAH-lumz) Tall, thin posts.

Congress (KON-gres) The part of the U.S. government that makes laws.

Constitution (kon-stih-TOO-shun) The basic rules by which the United States is governed.

conversations (kon-ver-SAY-shunz) Talks.

evolution (eh-vuh-LOO-shun) The way life on Earth has changed over many years.

filed (FY-uld) Officially brought something to court.

oath (OHTH) A promise.

retire (rih-TY-ur) To give up an office or other career.

Senate (SEH-nit) A law-making part of the U.S. government.

INDEX

WEB SITES

Due to the changing nature of Internet links, PowerKids Press has developed an online list of Web sites related to the subject of this book. This site is updated regularly. Please use this link to access the list:
www.powerkidslinks.com/hogw/justice/